This Book Belongs to
Jack Jackter Elementary
School   2004-2005

What Are
Screws?

by Helen Frost

Consulting Editor: Gail Saunders-Smith, Ph.D.

Consultant: Philip W. Hammer, Ph.D.
Assistant Director of Education
American Institute of Physics

Pebble Books

an imprint of Capstone Press
Mankato, Minnesota

Pebble Books are published by Capstone Press
151 Good Counsel Drive, P.O. Box 669, Mankato, Minnesota 56002
http://www.capstone-press.com

2 3 4 5 6 06 05 04 03 02

Library of Congress Cataloging-in-Publication Data
Frost, Helen, 1949–
    What are screws? / by Helen Frost.
        p. cm.—(Looking at simple machines)
    Includes bibliographical references (p. 23) and index.
    ISBN 0-7368-0848-5
    1. Screws—Juvenile literature. [1. Screws.] I.Title. II. Series.
TJ1338 .F68 2001
621.8′82—dc21

00-009868

Summary: Simple text and photographs present screws and their function as a
simple machine.

Note to Parents and Teachers

The Looking at Simple Machines series supports national science
standards for units on understanding work, force, and tools. This
book describes screws and illustrates how they make work easier.
The photographs support early readers in understanding the
text. This book also introduces early readers to subject-specific
vocabulary words, which are defined in the Words to Know section.
Early readers may need assistance to read some words and to use
the Table of Contents, Words to Know, Read More, Internet Sites,
and Index/Word List sections of the book.

Table of Contents

4

A screw is
a simple machine.

A screw is a rod
with a spiral around it.

thread

The spiral is called
the thread.

10

A screw can be turned with a small force.

The thread helps move the screw into an object.

Screws hold
objects together.

16

A bolt is
a kind of screw.

A lid is
a kind of screw.

A lightbulb is
a kind of screw.

Words to Know

force—a push or a pull on an object; force makes objects start moving, speed up, change direction, or stop moving.

screw—a rod with a thread around it; a screw is a simple machine that is used to hold objects together.

simple machine—a tool that makes work easier; work is using a force to move an object across a distance; inclined planes, levers, and pulleys are examples of simple machines; a screw is a type of inclined plane.

spiral—a pattern that goes around in circles; the spiral on a screw is an inclined plane.

thread—the spiral around a screw

Read More

Armentrout, Patricia. *The Screw.* Simple Devices. Vero Beach, Fla.: Rourke, 1997.

Glover, David. *Screws.* Simple Machines. Crystal Lake, Ill.: Rigby Interactive Library, 1997.

Rush, Caroline. *Slopes.* Simple Science. Austin, Texas: Raintree Steck-Vaughn, 1997.

Welsbacher, Anne. *Screws.* Understanding Simple Machines. Mankato, Minn.: Bridgestone Books, 2001.

Internet Sites

Inventor's Toolbox: The Elements of Machines
http://www.mos.org/sln/Leonardo/
InventorsToolbox.html

The Screw
http://www.fi.edu/qa97/spotlight3/screwdemo.html

Screws, Screws, and More Screws
http://weirdrichard.com:80/screw.htm

Simple Machines: Professor Beaker's Learning Labs
http://www.professorbeaker.com/simple.html

Index/Word List

around, 7
bolt, 17
force, 11
hold, 15
kind, 17, 19, 21
lid, 19
lightbulb, 21
machine, 5
move, 13

object, 13, 15
rod, 7
simple, 5
small, 11
spiral, 7, 9
thread, 9, 13
together, 15
turned, 11

Word Count: 65
Early-Intervention Level: 12

Editorial Credits
Martha E. H. Rustad, editor; Kia Bielke, cover designer and illustrator; Kimberly
    Danger, photo researcher

Photo Credits
Capstone Press/CG Book Printers, cover
David F. Clobes, 10, 12, 20
International Stock/Scott Campbell, 8
Kimberly Danger, 6, 18
Photo Agora/Jeff J. Daly, 16
Unicorn Stock Photos/Aneal Vohra, 1
Visuals Unlimited/Jack Ballard, 14

The author thanks the children's section staff at the Allen County Public Library
in Fort Wayne, Indiana, for research assistance. The author also thanks Josué
Njock Libii, Ph.D, Associate Professor of Mechanical Engineering at Indiana
University–Purdue University.